P9-DNH-600

FIGHT FOR RIGHTS

Written by

BARBARA WINTER

Illustrated by

DIMITRI KOSTIC

EMMELINE PANKHURST

CHRISTABEL PANKHURST

FLORA DUNCAN

THERESE GOULET

ADA TRENT

WILLIAM MARSH

MARY DUNCAN

REAL PEOPLE IN HISTORY

EMMELINE PANKHURST (1858–1928): She was a leader of the women's suffrage movement in England.

CHRISTABEL PANKHURST (1880–1958): Emmeline's daughter. She also campaigned for women's right to vote.

FICTIONAL CHARACTERS

MARY DUNCAN: A talented young girl who is drawn into the battle for women's suffrage.

FLORA DUNCAN: Mary's mother.

THERESE GOULET: A dressmaker who employs Mary in her dress shop.

ADA TRENT: An elderly shopkeeper who helps Mary and Flora.

WILLIAM MARSH: A young man who runs a cargo boat on the Thames River in London.

Contents

Christabel Pankhurst in England, shortly after her release from Holloway Prison, 1909

England

United States

For centuries, women all over the world were not allowed to vote in elections. They were considered inferior to men. Then, in the middle of the 19th century, women began to fight for the right to vote.

In Britain and the United States, the movement was known as women's suffrage. Suffrage means the right to vote. The people who fought in the movement were known as suffragists or suffragettes.

TIMELINE

1848 >>	1865 >>	1893 >>	1897 >>	1903 >>
The struggle for women's suffrage begins in the U.S.	Britain's first women's suffrage committee is formed in Manchester, England.	New Zealand is the first country to grant women the right to vote.	The National Union of Women's Suffrage is set up in England.	The Pankhursts start the Women's Social and Political Union in England.

Young girls at an American suffrage meeting, 1920

As women became educated, they realized they needed political power to improve the world around them. They wanted to change society by helping other women in areas like health, welfare, working conditions, and education.

At the end of the 19th century, the suffragists struggled very hard to make themselves heard. For some women, it was a matter of life and death.

WHAT'S THE STORY? This story is set in an actual time in history and depicts real people, but some of the characters and events are fictitious.

1913 »	1914 »	1918 »	1920 »	1928 »
The suffragist Emily Wilding Davison interrupts the Derby horse races in protest. She is injured and dies.	World War I interrupts the women's movement.	British women aged 30 and over are given the right to vote. Women in Canada are given the right to vote in federal elections.	Women in the U.S. gain the full right to vote.	Women in England are granted equal voting rights.

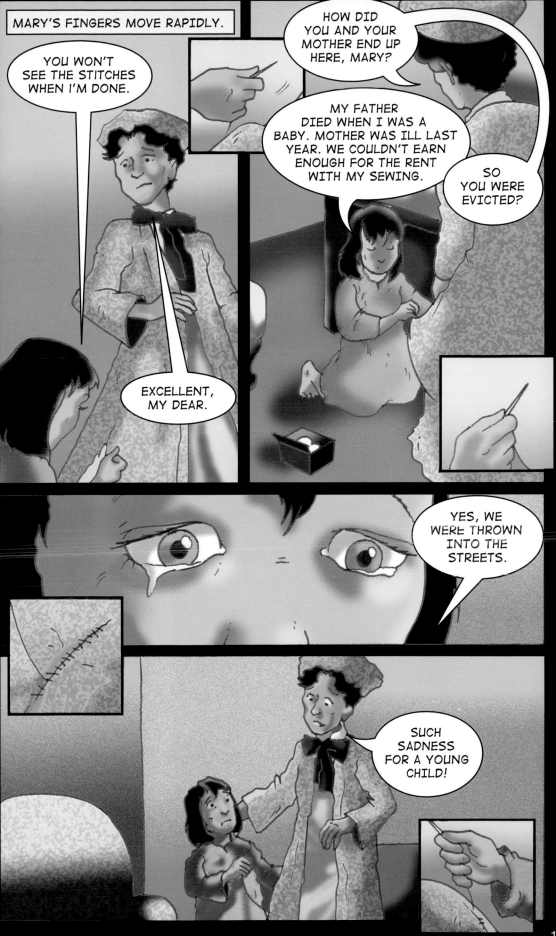

WORKHOUSES

Up until 1930 in Britain, people who could not afford to feed themselves were often sent to workhouses. These were institutions that provided work to people — orphans, widows, unmarried mothers, the old, and the sick — in return for meals and lodging. Workhouses were the last refuge of the desperate.

Life in the workhouse was made to be as harsh as possible so people would go there only when there was no other choice. Inmates were fed gruel (watery porridge) and they had to wear uniforms. Parents were separated from their children, and families were allowed to meet only on Sundays.

In the 1850s, concern grew over the poor living conditions in workhouses. In 1930, workhouses were abolished.

WOMEN'S SUFFRAGE

The fight for women's right to vote started in different countries in the 19th century. In the U.S., Elizabeth Cady Stanton and Lucretia Mott led the movement. Along with their belief in women's rights, they argued that slavery should be abolished. They also fought for African Americans to be given the vote.

In Britain, Emmeline Pankhurst and her daughter Christabel were outspoken suffragists. Strangely, Queen Victoria was opposed to the suffragists, even though she was a woman of power. It took almost 70 years for women to have the same voting rights as men.

New Zealand was the first country to grant suffrage to women in 1893. Australia followed in 1902, Canada in 1918, the U.S. in 1920, and Britain in 1928. There are still countries in the world where women are not considered fit to be given the vote. The struggle continues ...

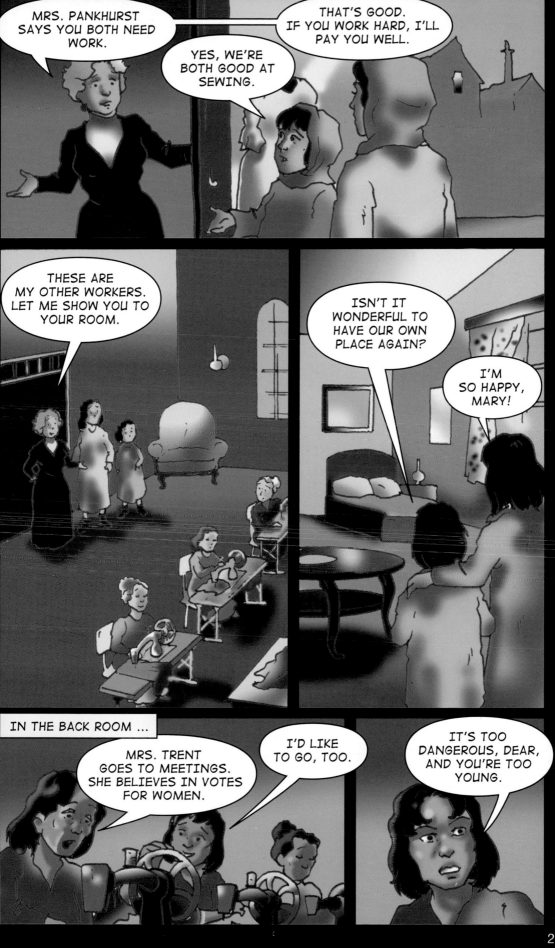

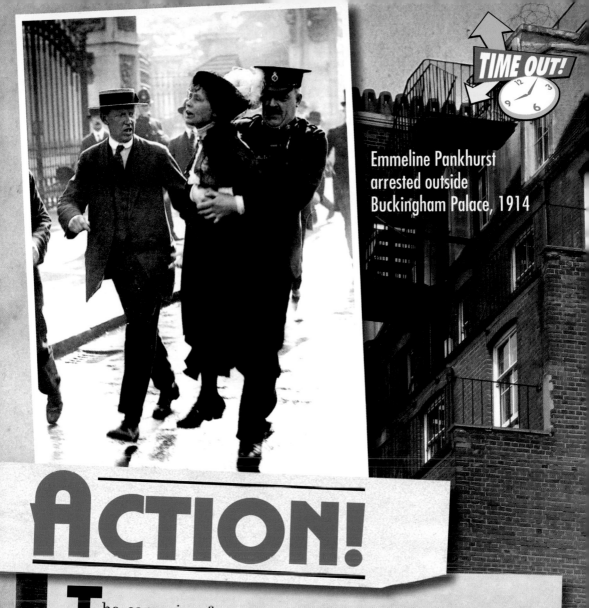

Emmeline Pankhurst
arrested outside
Buckingham Palace, 1914

ACTION!

The campaign for women's suffrage began in the 1860s. By the 1900s, women in Britain still could not vote in national elections. The newspapers lost interest in the matter. It became harder for suffragists to make themselves heard.

Emmeline and Christabel Pankhurst decided they had to do more to get attention. The suffragists created disturbances at public meetings. They broke the windows of government offices, and chained themselves to railings and lampposts. Some suffragists even set fire to public buildings!

By 1914, over 1,000 women had been sent to prison for destroying public property. Some suffragists disapproved of these violent tactics and withdrew from the movement. Many members of the public were also turned off by these acts.

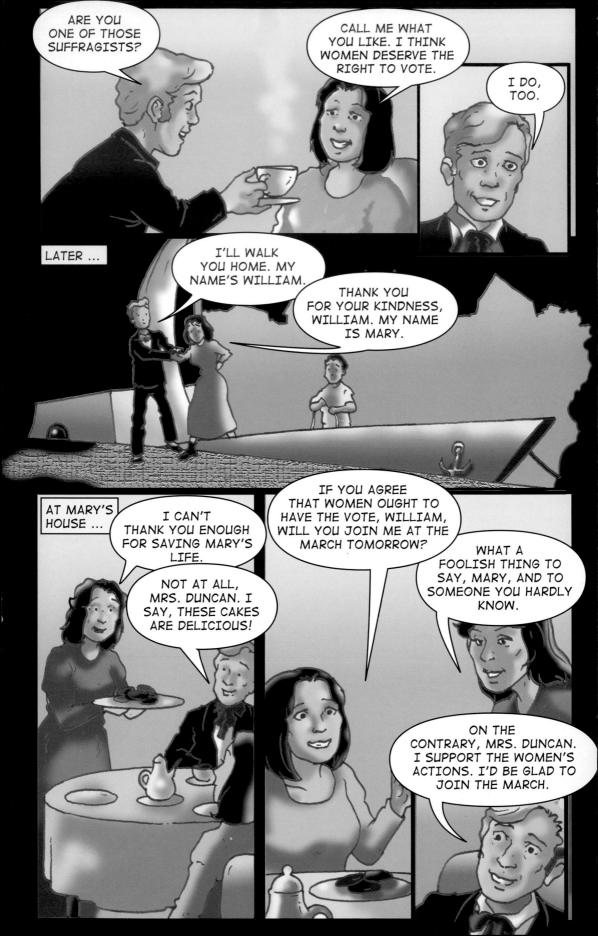

HUNGER STRIKE!

In 1909, one of the suffragists who had been sent to prison tried a new tactic: she refused to eat. By going on hunger strike and risking her life, she hoped to convince the public of the importance of her cause. Many women followed her example.

The government had a problem on its hands. If it allowed these women to die in prison, it might increase support for the suffragists. But if it released them, they would then be free to continue their acts of protest. Some women were force-fed.

The government came up with what became known as the Cat and Mouse Act. Under this act, they released women who became ill on hunger strikes, but as soon as they got well again, they were re-arrested.

Suffragists arrested outside Buckingham Palace in May, 1914

ATTENTION FOR THE CAUSE

At the Derby race, 1913

In her book *Unshackled — The Story of How We Won the Vote*, Christabel Pankhurst describes the shock she felt when she heard that Emily Wilding Davison had run in front of the king's horse at the Derby horse races. Here is an excerpt from the book, which was published in 1959, one year after Christabel's death:

> "Mother was ill from her second hunger-strike when there came the news of Emily Davison's historic act. She had stopped the King's horse at the Derby and was lying mortally injured. We were startled as everyone else. Not a word had she said of her purpose. Taking counsel with no one, she had gone to the racecourse, waited her moment, and rushed forward. Horse and jockey were unhurt, but Emily Davison paid with her life for making the whole world understand that women were in earnest for the vote. Probably in no other way and at no other time and place could she so effectively have brought the concentrated attention of millions to bear upon the cause."

WINNING

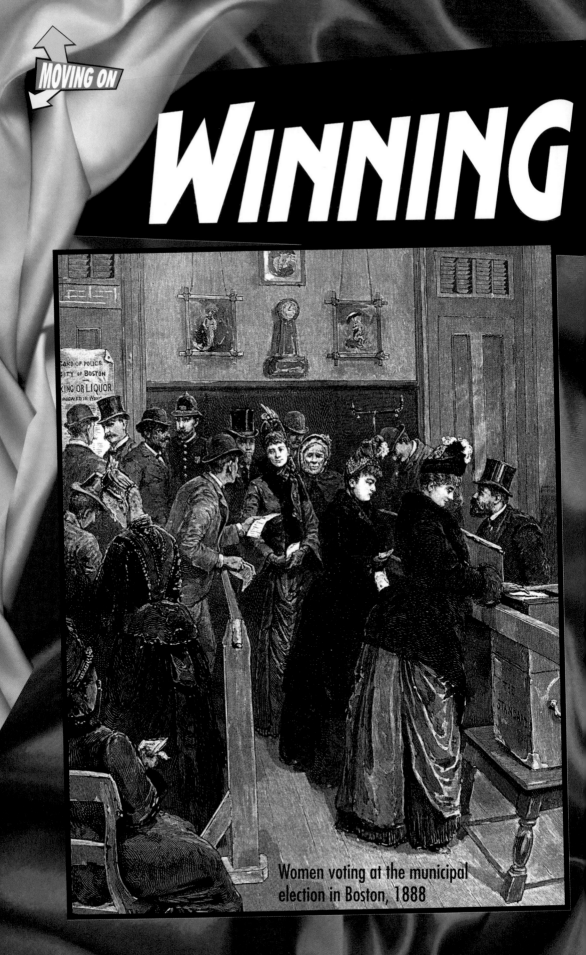

Women voting at the municipal
election in Boston, 1888

THE VOTE

Why was winning the vote so important to the suffragists? Was the cause really worth going to prison, starving oneself, or dying for?

In countries that practice democracy (rule by the people), citizens shape the society they live in by voting in elections. If there are social or political issues that people feel strongly about, they can express their opinions by voting. To be denied the right to vote is to be powerless.

The suffragists felt that it was wrong and unfair for women — at least half of any country's population — to be denied the vote. By the 19th century, many women were well educated and felt strongly about having a say in the way their countries were run.

Women were not the only people who had to fight for suffrage. In South Africa, for example, black people were not allowed to vote until the 1990s. There are still countries in the world where women and other groups are denied the right to vote.

INDEX

A
Annie, 22, 35–36
Australia, 21

B
Britain, 4, 13, 21, 29

C
Canada, 5, 21
Cat and Mouse Act, 36–37

D
Davison, Emily Wilding, 5, 39, 45
Democracy, 47
Derby horse races, 5, 35, 38, 45
Duncan, Flora, 30, 34, 35, 42
Duncan, Mary, 6, 8–9, 11–12, 14–16,
18–20, 22–23, 25–27, 31–32, 34, 36, 38,
42–44

E
Edward, King, 27, 38–39, 41, 45
England, 4–6, 40, 43

G
Germany, 40, 43
Goulet, Madame, 15–16, 18–19
Government, 26, 29, 36–37

H
Hyde Park, 25

L
Labour Party, 17

M
Marsh, William, 34–35, 38, 43–44
Matron, 7–10, 12, 14
Mott, Lucretia, 21
Movement, 4, 21, 29

N
National Union of Women's Suffrage, 4
New Zealand, 4, 21

P
Pankhurst, Christabel, 4, 15, 18–19,
21–22, 29, 35, 45
Pankhurst, Emmeline, 4, 8, 14, 16,
18–23, 29
Prime Minister, 24, 26
Protest, 20, 22, 37, 41

R
River Thames, 32

S
Stanton, Elizabeth Cady, 21
Suffrage, 4, 21, 25, 29, 47
Suffragists, 4–6, 21, 26, 29, 32, 34, 37,
40, 43, 47

T
Trent, Mr., 30
Trent, Mrs., 22–23, 27–28, 30–31, 41

U
United States of America, 4–5, 21

V
Victoria, Queen, 21
Vote, 4–5, 17–18, 20–21, 23–27, 29,
31–32, 34–35, 38, 40, 45, 47

W
Workhouse, 6–8, 12–13, 18